THE M. & E. COMPUTER

GW01158652

ELEMENTAI

ELEMENTARY ALGOL PROGRAMMING

ALAN BRUNDRITT
M.Sc., C.Eng., M.I.Struct.E.

Senior Lecturer, Department of Civil and Structural Engineering,
Faculty of Construction Technology and Design,
The Polytechnic of the South Bank

MACDONALD & EVANS LTD
8 John Street, London WC1N 2HY

MACDONALD & EVANS LTD.,
8 John Street, London WC1N 2HY
First published February 1976

MACDONALD AND EVANS LIMITED
1976

ISBN: 0 7121 0549 2

Phototypeset by Tradespools Ltd, Frome, Somerset
Printed in Great Britain by
Fletcher & Son Ltd, Norwich

General introduction

This series of books is directed primarily at those for whom this will be their first contact with computing and numerical analysis. The texts can therefore be used for a wide variety of courses in Science, Engineering and Mathematics (*e.g.* ONC, OND, Advanced Level, HNC, HND and Degree courses). The series at present comprises two books entitled *Elementary ALGOL* and *Elementary FORTRAN* and will shortly be extended to include a book on the BASIC computer language.

It is worth noting here that *Elementary FORTRAN* includes several chapters dealing in detail with those numerical methods used in computer programs with which the student should become familiar in order to write fairly simple but comprehensive scientific programs. The mathematical content of this book in fact follows that outlined in the syllabus for Paper III of the London Advanced Level in Pure Mathematics.

The increasing availability of hired remote terminals with direct access to a computer at a reasonable cost has meant that "the computer in the classroom" has become a reality and well within the budget of many schools and colleges. It is for those students who wish to make use of these and other computing facilities that these books have been written. The great advantage of using a direct access link in teaching a computing course is that the response is immediate and the system is largely self-teaching; it allows the student to correct, change and experiment with a program at a moment's notice.

Where access to a machine is not direct, programs are submitted, processed and returned perhaps the next day. One disadvantage of this system is that, if trivial errors occur frequently, the student may lose interest or even lose sight of the initial problem. If, however, he is determined to profit from his early errors, he will soon make rapid progress towards accurate and economical programming and also learn much about such topics as storage, running time and execution errors which have not been enlarged upon in these books.

Preface

Students wishing to know how or why a computer operates in the binary scale of numbers, or how the compiler works, or what comprises a computer installation or anything about the theory of electronics, will find that this book is of no use. However, students wishing to write a program (which will work) in the computer language ALGOL 60 or understand a program which someone else has written will find that the following pages are of interest and some use; they concentrate solely on programming in ALGOL. Later on, an ALGOL manual will be of considerable help because it is not claimed that everything that students need to know is to be found here.

ALGOL is a computer language which was conceived by an international committee and first published in 1960. Its name stands for "ALGOrithmic Language." The committee set out to design a new language and this was the first time that such a venture had been attempted. Their terms of reference were to produce a language which was independent of the machine operating it, was flexible, resembled a natural language and was problem-oriented—that is to say, the language can be adapted to the problem, rather than the problem altered to suit the available facilities of the language.

For detailed treatment of numerical methods used in computer programs, the reader is referred to *Elementary FORTRAN* by Dr. Petersen in the same series.

November 1975   A.B.

Contents

		page
	General Introduction	v
	List of Illustrations	ix
	Preface	xi
1.	Introduction	1
2.	The symbols of the language	2
3.	How do we write numbers?	4
4.	Identifiers	6
5.	Arithmetic expressions	8
6.	Assignment statements	10
7.	Special functions and words	13
8.	'goto' statements and labels	14
9.	'if' 'then' and 'if' 'then' 'else'	15
	Conditional assignment statement	
	Compound statements	
10.	Input	18
11.	Output	19
12.	Some simple programs	21
13.	Computer "errors"	28
14.	'for' statements	29
15.	Arrays	32
16.	More simple programs	37
17.	The **writetext** statement and page layout	45
18.	Boolean variables and expressions	48
19.	Procedures	50
20.	Here and there	55
	Integer division	
	Comment	
	'switch' declarations	
	entier(n)	
21.	Complete programs with data	60
	APPENDIX: Answers	63

List of illustrations

1. Flow diagram for Program 3.   24
2. Flow diagram for Program 4.   26
3. Flow diagram for Program 10.   41
4. Output using **writetext** statement.   46
5. Program to print prime numbers.   60
6. Program for a matrix calculation.   61

1
Introduction

It is essential to mention right from the outset a point in connection with the format of the book. In order to make a clear distinction between the programs (or parts of programs) written in ALGOL, and the accompanying explanatory text, the former have been set in lower-case bold type. Words which have a special significance and use in ALGOL are also so distinguished, even within the text. These latter are enclosed within apostrophes, which is the normal method (though by no means the only one) used to represent these words in a program processed by the 1900 series of I.C.L. computers. Where certain remarks apply only to the 1900 series, this is made clear in the text.

If you are not new to this subject you will surely realise that to go into detail on the subjects of basic ALGOL symbols and hardware representation would serve only to confuse the beginner; in addition, you will appreciate that the above paragraph is in places a deliberate over-simplification. Bear in mind, however, that my principal aim has been to present a text that is easy to understand, particularly when you read Chapters 2 and 7.

If you are a beginner, remember that you will not learn ALGOL or any other computer language just by reading this or any other book. You must write programs and attempt to run them on the computer. The compiler, which is part of the "works," will reproduce your program and tell you all the errors you have made (well, most of them). If a program is run unsuccessfully ten times, it will no doubt evoke some strong language from even the most patient programmer, but, believe me, there is no faster way to learn.

Good luck.

2
The symbols of the language

If we want to write any computer language, we must start by knowing what symbols we can use.

First, in ALGOL, we use the twenty-six letters of the English alphabet:

a b c d e f g h i j k l m n o p q r s t u v w x y z

(no Greek, Arabic, Hindustani or Chinese characters, if you please, with all due respect). Incidentally, when you write your program, you can use either capital or lower-case letters. That's up to you entirely. In fact, if you type them on an ordinary type-writer, the use of lower-case saves a lot of shift-key pressing, but the point to note is that the letter "a" is exactly the same as the letter "A." You cannot, on most computers, use these to represent two different quantities. When your program is reproduced, either on a Flexowriter (on which paper tape is punched), on a card-punching machine or on the computer printer itself, it will usually appear in capitals throughout.

Next, we have the nine digits and zero:

1 2 3 4 5 6 7 8 9 0

(Make sure that the letter I is not confused with the digit 1, nor zero with the letter O. It is normally clear from the context which symbol is intended.)

The following "operational" symbols are similar to those used in arithmetic or algebra:

+ Addition
− Subtraction
* Multiplication
/ Division
↑ "To the power of," the symbol of exponentiation

So are the symbols indicating certain relations:

= equal to
≠ not equal to

$<$ less than
$>$ greater than
'le' less than or equal to
'ge' greater than or equal to

And lastly some punctuation symbols are used:

$$. \quad , \quad : \quad ; \quad ' \quad (\quad)$$

You may have thought it unnecessary even to mention these, but in writing ALGOL they are vitally important. Omission or misuse of a single comma may mean your program is doomed. We shall examine the precise use of these symbols very shortly.

There are a few other symbols, but the ones already given are enough for our present purposes.

3
How do we write numbers?

There are two types of number in ALGOL:

'integer' and **'real'**

An **'integer'** is a positive or negative whole number, *e.g.*:

57   − 6   12345   − 2001   498170

A **'real'** number has a decimal portion, *e.g.*:

215·34   − 67·89   − 0·00004

(Note that the zero before the decimal point is not essential. Its use here is purely a personal preference.)

Another form of expression for **'real'** numbers is the mantissa and exponent form, commonly met in the display or print-out of smaller computers, *e.g.*:

2·1534 & 2   **− 6·789 & 1**   **− 4 & − 5**

The ampersand (**&**) means "times ten to the power of." These last examples give the same numbers as the **'real'** numbers first shown above.

It is unlikely that you will often want to use the mantissa and exponent form, when it is just as simple and probably clearer to use the normal decimal form. Numbers may take this form however either in a program or on a data card or tape. (We shall deal later with the subject of data, *see* Chapters 10 and 12.)

It is necessary at this point to mention a few "don'ts":

1. Do not use an **'integer'** whose numerical value is greater than 8388607. The computer cannot hold a larger one. Why this number? Well, it happens to be $2^{23} - 1$ so since the computer works in the scale of 2 it indicates that there are 24 circuits to a number location.

2. Do not use a **'real'** number whose numerical value is greater than **5·6 & 76** (the reason is similar). I can't think why you should need to—if you're going space-travelling I suggest you get a bigger computer.

3. You must not use a non-integral exponent after **&**. For instance, the number **2·3 & 1·67** is not valid.

4. Never end a number with the decimal point. There must be at least one digit after it (*e.g.*: **50·0, 0·0**).

NOTE: The limitations in 1 and 2 above apply to machines in the 1900 series.

There are many further points to be noted about numbers, but it might be better to introduce them gradually as we proceed and as they need to be understood.

Now see if you can decide which of the following numbers are acceptable to the computer:

(*a*) **− 406**	(*g*) **1**
(*b*) **8412000**	(*h*) **17 & 1·5**
(*c*) **2·75 & − 6**	(*i*) **648·123456**
(*d*) **5· & 3**	(*j*) **920·**
(*e*) **0·00**	(*k*) **4·92 & − 77**
(*f*) **21·0**	(*l*) **·123**

4
Identifiers

Before a computer can carry out calculations it must obviously have some numbers to work on. These are placed in certain "locations." You may like to think of them as small boxes, although in fact they are electrical circuits. Let the electronics chaps worry about these. We don't have to.

These boxes have to be given names so that we can tell the computer which we are referring to. The name of a box is called an *identifier*. This idea is exactly similar to the way we denote variables in algebra by using single letters.

A valid identifier is any group of letters and/or digits (but *no* other symbols) provided that the group *does not commence with a digit*. For example:

a   x2   bm   fred   p25f   abracadabra

are all perfectly valid identifiers. (The last one is not recommended. It takes too long to type or punch.)

You will find after a time that **fred** and **daphne** and **kplonk** are a bit of a drag and that you will prefer to use as identifiers names which suggest to you the quantities they represent, *e.g.*:

volume   area   sum   voltage   force

or perhaps some shortened version of these.

Due to the way the computer's printing device works. *i.e.* line by line, there can be no provision for letters or digits to be written superscript or subscript. Therefore,

$$i_{xx} \qquad x^2 \qquad r_{b2}$$

are not valid. They cannot be reproduced like this, anyway.

When the computer "reads" your program it will take no notice of blank spaces between letters or numbers nor the change to a new line. It will read the characters in strict sequence as it comes to them. So, at the risk of being considered somewhat

6

eccentric, you could write the identifier **axisdepth** in this fashion:

$$
\begin{array}{lll}
\text{a} & \text{xi} & \\
\quad\text{s} & \text{de} & \text{p} \\
\quad\text{t} & \text{h} & \\
\end{array}
$$

The computer will be quite happy to cope with this, but I don't imagine anyone reading it will.

You should now have no difficulty in deciding which of the following are valid identifiers:

(*a*)	**3root**	(*j*)	**barbara**
(*b*)	**mid-span**	(*k*)	π **d**
(*c*)	**z(yy)**	(*l*)	**a2f45p**
(*d*)	**mid span**	(*m*)	**cos** α
(*e*)	**ryy**	(*n*)	**cc 2**
(*f*)	**piedee**	(*o*)	**co-efficient**
(*g*)	**identifier**	(*p*)	**blast !**
(*h*)	**co·ord**	(*q*)	**a1b2c3d4**
(*i*)	**s p a n**	(*r*)	**voltage drop**

5
Arithmetic expressions

These are written much as in ordinary algebra. There are, however, one or two points which should be noted carefully.

1. The multiplication sign must always be expressed, not implied as it so often is in algebra. For instance:

abc must be written   **a * b * c**

$4ei/s$ must be written   **4 * e * i / s**

If the asterisks were to be omitted, the computer would simply read the expressions abc and $4ei$ as if they were single identifiers. (In the latter case, as you now know, the identifier would be declared invalid because it commences with a digit.)

2. In dealing with expressions which contain several different operational symbols, the computer has an order of priority:

1st: ↑
2nd: *   /
3rd: +   −

The signs are dealt with according to this order. Thus:

$$a + b ↑ 2 / 7 \quad \text{will give} \quad a + \frac{b^2}{7}$$

$$m ↑ n − p * 2 \quad \text{will give} \quad m^n − 2p$$

If the expression contains signs of equal priority, these will be dealt with as the computer meets them, reading from left to right. Thus:

a * b / c   will give ab/c

a / b * c / d   will give ac/bd

3. Round brackets (and *only* round ones) have their normal algebraic function and may be freely used, even if not strictly necessary, to make the intention clear.

a / bc becomes   **a / (b * c)**

8

$$\frac{b^2 - 4ac}{2a} \qquad \text{becomes} \qquad \textbf{(b} \boldsymbol{\uparrow} \textbf{2} - \textbf{4} * \textbf{a} * \textbf{c)} / \textbf{(2} * \textbf{a)}$$

$$\frac{m^{-n} + y}{m + n} \qquad \text{becomes} \qquad \textbf{(m} \boldsymbol{\uparrow} \textbf{(} - \textbf{n)} + \textbf{y)} / \textbf{(m} + \textbf{n)}$$

Note particularly, in the last example, the brackets round $(- \textbf{n})$. These are essential because it is a rule that two operational symbols may not be placed together.

Try to write the following expressions correctly in ALGOL.

(a) $a^3 + 2a - 7$

(b) $\left(\dfrac{p + q}{2}\right)^2 + 4r^2$

(c) $\dfrac{x + 3(x^2 - 7)}{(2y + 1)^3}$

(d) $a (1 - a)(1 + a - a^2)$

(e) $f \Big/ \left[1 + \dfrac{1}{6000}\left(\dfrac{L}{k}\right)^2\right]$

(f) $(a^x + a^{-x}) / 2$

6
Assignment statements

We said earlier that in order to put numbers into the computer we give a name, an identifier, to a box. How do we now tell the computer that a certain box is to have a certain numerical value? By an *assignment statement*, *e.g.*:

$$w := 20 \cdot 58 \ ;$$

This statement is usually read as:

                w becomes equal to 20·58
or   set **w** equal to 20·58

On receiving this instruction, the computer will allocate to the location named **w** the number 20·58. If **w** has already been given a value, this statement will wipe out the previous value and substitute the new value 20·58.

$$x := a * b \ ;$$

In this instance the computer will allocate to the location **x** the product of the numbers in locations **a** and **b**.

The following rules for writing assignment statements should be noted:

1. Every complete statement must terminate with a semicolon (;).

2. If you leave out the colon (:) (a very common error) and just write:

$$w = 20 \cdot 58$$

you are simply telling the computer that the value of **w** is 20·58 which it presumably knows. You are not *instructing it to do anything*. The expression $w = 20 \cdot 58$ is not a statement, but a relation and, as we shall see shortly may be used in conjunction with the word '**if**'.

3. The left-hand side of an assignment statement can be only a single identifier. The statement $x + 2 \cdot 3 := 5 * y$ would be utter rubbish, rather like telling the barmaid, "Please put my bitter into a silver tankard minus seven"!

If we wish to assign to more than one variable the same numerical value, this can be done by a *multiple assignment statement.*

Before an example of a multiple assignment statement is given, it is necessary to explain that, at the commencement of any program, we have to tell the computer what variable names we intend to use and also whether these variables are going to represent **'integer'** or **'real'** numbers. Now, all the variables in a multiple assignment statement must have been declared to be of the same type. Thus, if **x** and **y** have been declared as **'integer'**, we can say:

$$x := y := 50 ;$$

Each of the variables **x** and **y** is assigned the value 50.

Similarly, supposing the variables **a**, **b** and **vol** to have been declared **'real'**:

$$a := b := vol := 3 \cdot 56 ;$$

It would be natural at this point to ask the effect of assigning a decimal number to an **'integer'** variable and vice versa. In order to answer this question, it is appropriate to explain that the computer actually performs its calculations, not in the decimal system, but in the scale of two (the binary scale). It is not really necessary to go into the details of this subject. Suffice it to say that if any calculation involving whole numbers yields a whole number answer, then in any scale this will be calculated exactly. If not, the answer will be computed to as great a degree of accuracy as we should need.

If we assign a whole number, say 56, to an **'integer'** variable and have it printed in **'integer'** form, we will get the exact result, 56. If, however, we assign it to a **'real'** variable, and print it in **'real'** form, it will appear to a certain number of decimal places, *e.g.*:

$$56 \cdot 0 \qquad \text{or} \qquad 56 \cdot 0000$$

There is no difficulty here.

If, however, we have a decimal result and assign it to an **'integer'** variable, it is assigned as the *nearest whole number.* (This occurs even before it is printed.) Clearly, this could be annoying, even disastrous to our calculation. For instance, suppose that we intend to divide by a number which has the value $0 \cdot 35$ and we have inadvertently assigned this to an **'integer'**. It is assigned as zero (the nearest whole number). The computer is programmed to record an "overflow" error when asked to divide by zero, and the program stops.

This difficulty can be resolved by adopting a simple rigid rule.

If in your program a variable is *by nature* a whole number (*e.g.* one used to count a number of operations or a number of numbers) then declare it as an **'integer'**. If it is, or could be, decimal then declare it as **'real'**.

Now try some simple exercises in using assignment statements:

(*a*) Assuming in the following examples that the variables **a**, **b** and **c** have been declared **'integer'** and **x**, **y** and **z** are **'real'**, what will be the values assigned to these variables?

> (*i*)   **a := 4 + 5/3 ;**
> (*ii*) **b := 6 * 2·4 ;**
> (*iii*) **c := 2/4 ↑ 3 ;**
> (*iv*) **x := 7 * 13 * 1·1 ;**
> (*v*)   **y := 240/6/5/5 ;**
> (*vi*) **z := 27 ↑ (−2/3) ;**

(*b*) After the following series of statements has been obeyed, what are the values of **a** and **b**?

$$a := b := 4 ;$$
$$a := a + b ;$$
$$b := a + b ;$$
$$a := a + b ;$$

(*c*) As a final exercise, let us imagine that you wish to interchange the positions of two numbers in the computer. You write:

$$m := 7 ; n := 4 ;$$
$$n := m ;$$
$$m := n ;$$

(*i*) What has gone wrong, and (*ii*) what is the simplest way of effecting the interchange?

7
Special functions and words

There are many common mathematical functions which we find useful in calculations, such as the trigonometric functions of sine and cosine, the square root or the exponential logarithm.

The computer holds many of these functions as built-in programs or subroutines. Here is a list of some of the most common. The value on which the computer operates (generally called the *parameter* or *argument* of the function) must always be enclosed within round brackets. Each of the items in this list may be used in just the same way as a number or expression on the right-hand side of an assignment statement.

sin (a)	sine of *a*	*a* being in radians.
cos (a)	cosine of *a*	
abs (x)	the absolute value of *x*, *i.e.* its positive numerical value.	
ln(y)	log *y* to the base *e*.	
sqrt (p)	the positive square root of *p*.	
exp (q)	*e* to the power of *q*.	
arctan (m)	the angle (in radians) whose tangent is *m*.	

Some examples:

$$t := \sin(x) / \cos(x) ;$$
$$hypot := \mathrm{sqrt}\,(a * a + b * b) ;$$
$$angle := \arctan\,(\sin(theta)/\cos(theta)) ;$$
$$r := \ln\,(\mathrm{abs}(x) - \mathrm{abs}(x/2));$$

As mentioned in the Preface, certain words have a special meaning and use in ALGOL and are normally distinguished by being placed in single quotation marks. We have already come across: **'integer' 'real' 'le' 'ge'**. Here are a few more which we shall meet in the course of the next few chapters.

'begin' 'end' 'if' 'then' 'else' 'goto'
'and' 'or' 'for' 'step' 'until' 'while'

8
'goto' statements and labels

The computer normally executes statements in strict sequence, but we may sometimes wish to depart from this sequence and jump forward or backward to some other point in the program. This is done by means of a **'goto'** statement and the use of a label. Look at the following short portion of a program:

$$x := 0 \ ;$$
$$y := 0 \ ;$$
again: $\quad x := x + 1 \ ;$
$$y := y + 2 * x \ ;$$
$$\textbf{'goto' again} \ ;$$

x and y are first given initial values of zero. x is now increased by 1 and y increased by twice the value of x. The computer is now told to go to the statement labelled **again :** Now x is again increased by 1 and y by twice the value of x. So the process is repeated. Until when? Well, in this instance, until the computer tells you in no uncertain fashion that your time is up and others are waiting to use the machine! This situation we call an *endless loop*. Naturally our programs must try to avoid them. All the same, they often happen accidentally, and the reason is not always as obvious as it is here.

Note that a label can be any valid identifier and is always followed by a colon (:). Also note that a label encountered during the normal sequential execution of statements is simply overrun by the computer (as would happen in the above example the first time through).

9
'if' 'then' and 'if' 'then' 'else'

We shall often want the computer to perform an operation only on condition that some relation is true. The form of the **'if' 'then'** statement is more or less that used in basic English, *e.g.*:

$$\text{'if' } x = 0 \text{ 'then' } y := y + 2;$$

When this instruction is met the computer will find out whether $x = 0$. If so, it will carry out the instruction $y := y + 2$; If not, the **'then'** portion will be completely ignored and the computer will proceed to the *next statement*.

Further examples:

$$\text{'if' } bm > 60 \text{ 'then' 'goto' } zz;$$

(**zz:** will be a label elsewhere in the program.)

$$\text{'if' } abs(x) \text{ 'le' } 1 \cdot 0 \text{ 'then' } x := 0;$$

Now suppose that we wish the computer to take one of two alternative actions. Once again, the form of the statement is fairly straightforward.

$$\text{'if' } y > 0 \text{ 'then' } x := sqrt(y) \text{ 'else' 'goto' } neg;$$

In this instance, if **y** is greater than zero, **x** will be put equal to the square root of **y** (and the remainder of the statement ignored). If **y** is not greater than zero (*i.e.* is less than or equal to zero) the **'then'** portion will be disregarded and the **'else'** portion obeyed, and a jump will occur to the label **neg:**

Note carefully that the word **'else'** must *never* be preceded by a semicolon. The **'if' 'then' 'else'** form is a complete single statement.

If three or more alternatives exist the statement can be extended to any length in the following manner:

$$\text{'if' } t = 1 \text{ 'then' } s := 0 \text{ 'else' 'if' } t = 2 \text{ 'then'}$$
$$s := -6 \text{ 'else' 'goto' } recalc;$$

15

or perhaps:

> 'if' x > y 'then' n := ('if' z = 0 'then' 2 'else' 4)
> 'else' 'if' x = y 'then' m := 1 'else' 'goto' waterloo ;

Some can be quite complicated, can't they? Better read that last one again slowly.

Conditional assignment statement

This has already been used in the last example above. It assigns two or more alternative values to a variable. A simple example is:

$$x := \text{'if'} \ y = 3 \ \text{'then'} \ 4 \ \text{'else'} \ 0 \ ;$$

x is assigned the value 4 or zero depending on the value of y.

Note that, in this type of assignment statement, the **'if' 'then' 'else'** form must be used. It would be invalid to say:

$$a := \text{'if'} \ x = 3 \ \text{'then'} \ 0 \ ;$$

because the computer is left "in the air" if x is not equal to 3. It would be tantamount to saying:

$$a :=$$

and that is not much use!

Compound statements

It often happens that, depending on the result of a decision, we may wish to instruct the computer to perform not just one but many statements. If so, then these statements must be enclosed in a special type of "brackets." The brackets are formed by the words **'begin'** and **'end'** enclosing the "compound statement."

For example:

> 'if' b = a * c 'then'
> 'begin' b := 0 ;
>   a := a + f ;
>   c := c ↑ 2 ;
>   'goto' nextnumber
> 'end' ;

If the **'begin'** and **'end'** were omitted in this sequence, then only the statement **b := 0 ;** would be conditional on the **'if'** statement. The subsequent statements, **a := a + f ;** etc., would then be executed in any case.

You will notice that in this example no semicolon precedes the word **'end'** ; It is not necessary, but it is not wrong to put one, and some like to play safe by inserting it.

Another example:

> **'if' t = 2 'or' t = 4 'then' 'goto' result**
> **'else'**
> **'begin' t := t + 1 ;**
>   **'goto' again**
> **'end' ;**

In this example we have introduced the word **'or'**. This means exactly what it does in English. The word **'and'** can be used in a similar situation, in which case both relations which it connects have to be satisfied. If you used **'and'** to replace **'or'** in the above example, what would happen?

Note once again that no semicolon precedes the word **'else'**.

10
Input

It is not usual to assign numerical values to the variables within the program, because we may want to run the same program with many different sets of numerical values. We normally write our program setting out the various mathematical operations to be performed and then, following the program, provide the computer with a list of numbers on which to operate. Such a list is known as *data* or the *input stream*.

The statement:

$$a := read \ ;$$

instructs the computer to take the next number from the input stream and assign it to the variable **a**.

This word, **read**, is an internal function rather like **cos (a)**, except that it needs no parameter (and therefore no round brackets). It can be used as if it were a variable in such expressions as:

sum := **sum** + **read** ;
term := **6** * **read** + **4** ;   etc.

Each time the word **read** is encountered, the next item on the input stream is inserted into the statement and treated as instructed.

11
Output

When the computer has calculated the results that we want, we must instruct it to print them. One form of output statement, the most common, is:

$$\textbf{print } (p, m, n) \text{ ;}$$

where p indicates the variable whose value is to be printed. It may be a single variable or any arithmetic expression. m and n are positive integers or zero.

Once again, **print** is an internal function (to give it its correct name, it is a **'procedure'**) and is followed in round brackets by three parameters, p, m and n, which as you will notice must be separated by commas. There is no comma after the last parameter.

The possible values of m and n produce three permutations:

1. $m \neq 0, n = 0$.

This will output an **'integer'** with m digits, which will be prefixed by a negative sign if appropriate. For example:

print (a, 4, 0) ; · Output:	**6704**
	−9572

2. $m \neq 0, n \neq 0$.

This outputs a **'real'** number with m digits before the decimal point and n digits after it. For example:

print (n, 3, 3) ; Output:	**−872·169**
	445·008

3. $m = 0, n \neq 0$.

The output in this case is in "floating point" form. This is a name given to the mantissa and exponent notation already mentioned (*see* Chapter 3). Again this gives n digits after the decimal point in the mantissa. For example:

print (x, 0, 4) ; Output:	**1·7236 & −2**
	−9·7251 & 16

Two questions will probably spring to mind. Suppose the number to be printed has fewer digits before the decimal point than has been stipulated in the instruction, what then? and suppose it has more?

There is no difficulty. The parameters m and n reserve an appropriate number of spaces for the result and provided that the number contains *up to m* digits before the decimal point it will appear, immediately preceded by a negative sign where necessary, in the space so provided.

For instance, let us imagine that we are printing a column of results and have used the format **print(z,4,2) ;** We might get the following print-out:

$$4536 \cdot 12$$
$$-786 \cdot 66$$
$$2 \cdot 01$$
$$-1234 \cdot 56$$
$$-43555 \cdot 17$$

This list illustrates the answer to both queries above. The last number shows what happens when the number is greater than the format allowed for. You will get the answer correctly printed but the neat setting-out has been disturbed. So try to estimate the largest number you expect to get and arrange the format accordingly.

It might be worth mentioning here exactly what space is taken up by the **print** instruction. In the following examples it is assumed that the number being printed contains the maximum number of digits expressed in the format.

For **'integer'** numbers	x**1234**xx
For **'real'** numbers	x**1234·567**xx

The initial x here denotes the space reserved for the negative sign where required and the two final x symbols denote blank spaces. Thus, an **'integer'** occupies $m + n + 3$ spaces and a **'real'** $m + n + 4$ spaces.

12
Some simple programs

We are now in a position to compose some simple programs which you can run on the computer.

Program 1

Read in any numbers (each less than 100) in pairs, *a* and *b*, calculate the values of the expressions:

$$2a^3 - 6a^2 + 10a - 3$$

and $\qquad\qquad 7b^2 + 4b - 16$

Print the two values and also their product, and if the product is positive, print its square root also. The data is to terminate with a number exceeding 100.

```
'begin'
      'real' a, b, p, x, y ;
nextpair:  a := read ;
            'if' a > 100 'then' 'goto' stop ;
            b := read ;
            x := 2 * a↑3 − 6 * a↑2 + 10 * a − 3 ;
            y := 7 * b↑2 + 4 * b − 16 ;
            p := x * y ;
            print (x,4,3) ; print (y,4,3) ;
            print(p,6,3) ;
            'if' p > 0·0 'then' print(sqrt(p),4,3) ;
            newline(1) ;
            'goto' nextpair ;
stop:
'end' ;
```

There are several points to be noted in this program so read the following carefully.

NOTES:
  1. The whole program must be enclosed by **'begin'** and **'end'**;
  2. After the initial **'begin'** we first declare what variables will

21

be used and of what type they are. The computer can recognise an **'integer'** or **'real'** number by its form, but it has to be told what type a variable is.

3. Labels do not have to be declared.

4. Each pair of numbers is read in to variables **a** and **b**. Note that the value of **a** is tested before **b** is read. If we had read the pair **a** and **b** and then tested **a**, think what would have happened when we reached the value used as the terminator. This would have been assigned to **a** and there would be no number to assign to **b**. An error would be recorded due to insufficient data. In this particular instance the error would occur after we had obtained the results required but it is not good practice to let a program fail in this way. So, when **a** is read as a number greater than 100, the program proceeds as instructed to the label **stop:** and concludes as intended.

5. The statement **newline(1)** moves the printer mechanism to the next line.

6. Since this program is written in a general form so that any pairs of numbers may be processed, we now provide a list of data on which the computer is to operate. It will be remembered from Chapter 4 that normally the computer ignores any spaces and any change to a new line (or new card). It will also be clear that if this applied to a list of numbers, and the numbers were presented thus:

$$4 \ 32 \ 67 \ 8 \cdot 5$$

the computer would read this as the number 432678·5. So slightly different rules apply to the preparation of data on tape or on cards. When "reading" data, the computer recognises the end of a number as soon as it encounters:

(*a*) at least *two* spaces;

(*b*) a comma;

(*c*) a semicolon; or

(*d*) the keyboard character representing a new line (if the program is on tape) or when it reads a new card (if the program is on cards).

Suppose we supply three pairs of numbers followed by a number above 100 as a terminator; each of the following is a valid form for the data:

$$2 \cdot 6 \quad -3 \quad 10 \cdot 5 \quad -7 \cdot 65 \quad 2 \cdot 1 \quad 15 \cdot 34$$
$$101$$

$$2 \cdot 6, -3, 10 \cdot 5, -7 \cdot 65$$
$$2 \cdot 1; 15 \cdot 34; 101$$

7. It might be noticed in passing that in ALGOL each statement does not need to appear on a new line or card. The semicolon indicates the end of each complete statement.

Program 2

Calculate and print the areas of circles and volumes of spheres for radii from 1 unit to 20 units inclusive. (Area $= \pi r^2$; volume $= \frac{4}{3}\pi r^3$.)

```
'begin' 'integer' r ;
        'real' pi ;
        pi := 4 * arctan(1) ;  r := 0 ;
next:   r := r + 1 ;
        print(pi  *  r  *  r, 4, 3) ; space(10) ;
        print(4 * pi * r↑3 / 3, 5, 3) ;
        newline(1) ;
        'if' r < 20 'then' 'goto' next
'end' ;
```

NOTES:
1. We could have assigned to the variable **pi** the value 3·142 or 3·14159, etc. The method shown gives the value of π to the maximum accuracy of the computer. A useful tip to remember.
2. The statement **space(10)** ; instructs the computer printer to move ten blank spaces along the line.

Program 3

Discover all the numbers less than 10000 which are simultaneously square and triangular. (A triangular number is defined as the sum of the first n natural numbers, e.g.:

$$
\begin{matrix}
 & & & & & & \cdot \\
 & & \cdot & & & \cdot & \cdot \\
\cdot & & \cdot & \cdot & & \cdot & \cdot & \cdot \\
1 & & 3 & & & 6 & & & \text{etc.)}
\end{matrix}
$$

For many types of program it is helpful to set out a *flow diagram*. This is a logical summary of the main steps to be taken. from which the program can later be built up. A flow diagram for this program is shown in Fig. 1.

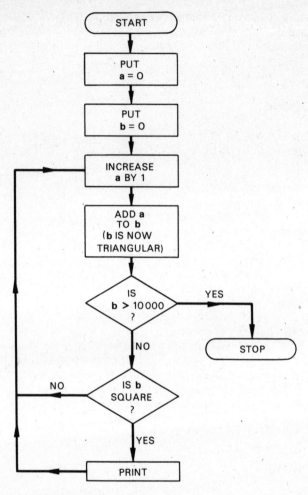

FIG. 1. Flow diagram for Program 3.

When we are satisfied that the logic and routing are correct, we can translate the steps into ALGOL.

```
'begin' 'integer' a, b, c ;
        a := b := 0 ;
again:  a := a + 1 ;
        b := b + a ;
        'if' b > 10000 'then' 'goto' stop ;
        c := sqrt(b) ;
```

```
        'if' c * c = b 'then' print(b, 5, 0) ;
        'goto' again ;
  stop :
  'end' ;
```

NOTES:

1. Note the comma separators between the variables in the declaration at the beginning.

2. To find out whether a number is square, we take its square root and assign it to an **'integer'** variable, **c**. If **b** is not an exact square then **c** will be rounded off to the nearest whole number. Then **c * c** will not give **b**.

In a similar vein, you may care to find a number which is simultaneously square and square pyramidal. (A square pyramidal number is defined as the sum of the squares of the first n natural numbers, *e.g.* 1, 5, 14, 30, etc.)

Incidentally it has been proved that there is only one such number. It is less than 10000. Be very careful that your program stops at 10000, otherwise the computer will search in vain.

Program 4

Determine the sum of the series:

$$1 + \tfrac{1}{4} + \tfrac{1}{9} + \tfrac{1}{16} + \cdots$$

neglecting all terms less than 10^{-8}.

Once again a flow diagram may be helpful (*see* Fig. 2).

```
  'begin' 'integer' n ; 'real' term, sum ;
        n := 0 ; sum := 0·0 ;
  next :  n := n + 1 ;
        term := 1/(n * n) ;
        'if' term < & −8 'then' 'goto' out ;
        sum := sum + term ;
        'goto' next ;
  out :    print(sum,1,6)
  'end' ;
```

Note here the use of the ampersand (**&**) without a preceding number. **& −8** signifies simply 10 to the power of −8.

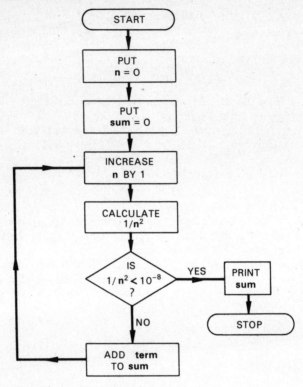

FIG. 2. Flow diagram for Program 4.

Program 5

In a computer staff beauty contest, finalists are to be chosen according to the following rules:

1. Height must be between 5 ft 4 in and 5 ft 8 in inclusive.
2. Bust and hip measurements must not differ by more than 2 in.
3. Hip and waist measurements must not differ by less than 11 in.

Read in, for an unstated number of contestants, the height and vital statistics as integral numbers of inches. Print the number of each finalist followed by her measurements and count and print the number of successful finalists. An impossibly large height is to be used as the data terminator.

```
'begin' 'integer' n, f, ht, h, w, b ;
        n := f := 0 ;
```

```
again : n := n + 1 ;
        ht := read ; 'if' ht > 80 'then' 'goto' stop ;
        b := read ; w := read ; h := read ;
        'if' ht < 64 'or' ht > 68 'then' 'goto' again ;
        'if' abs(b − h) > 2 'then' 'goto' again ;
        'if' h − w < 11 'then' 'goto' again ;
        f := f + 1 ;
        print(n, 2, 0) ; space(10) ;
        print(ht, 2, 0) ; space(5) ;
        print(b, 2, 0) ; print(w, 2, 0) ;
        print(h, 2, 0) ; newline(1) ;
        'goto' again ;
stop :  newline(1) ; print(f, 2, 0)
'end' ;
```

NOTES:

1. **n** counts the contestants.

2. **f** counts the accepted finalists and is incremented only if the contestant is not rejected by any of the **'if'** statements.

3. The data stream will consist of a number of sets of four numbers followed by a number greater than 80 as terminator.

13
Computer "errors"

This seems a convenient place to take a "breather." Let us leave the technical side for a moment and digress a little.

From certain remarks one hears, it is clear that the computer has developed a bad reputation in some quarters—"Computers? Wouldn't touch 'em." "Sorry, Madam, but your bill is due to a computer error."

It is felt that such remarks arise from misconceptions as to what a computer is and does, so let us get one point straight. The computer is, amongst other rather more complimentary things, a high-speed idiot. It can only do (albeit at an incredible speed) what it is instructed to do by a human being. Generally speaking it does it perfectly. If you do not get the answers which you expected, and to use a computer with intelligence we ought to know roughly what these are, the odds are that you have not told it to do what you thought you had.

Of course, being a machine, the computer can develop mechanical troubles and, when this happens, either you will get no results or your results will be quite obviously wrong and immediately detectable. But during the course of several years' experience the author has found very few cases in which an error has not been traced eventually to a slip in the programming.

In one of A. A. Milne's delightful books, Christopher Robin observes of his friend Pooh:

> And if HE's right, I'M right,
> And if HE's wrong, it isn't ME.

Believe me, as far as the computer is concerned, if he's wrong, it probably *is* you!

14
'for' statements

Look again at Program 2 in Chapter 12 and note the method used to form a "loop." Such a loop requires four essential conditions:

1. The variable must be assigned an initial value.

2. The variable must be increased by 1 at the beginning of each loop.

3. The start of the loop must be labelled.

4. The current value of the variable has to be tested each time round to see if the loop has been performed the required number of times.

A 'for' statement does all these things in a much neater way, and is one of the most powerful and versatile of ALGOL devices. Look at one simple example, which once again is almost of the form used in basic English.

'for' i := 1 'step' 1 'until' 50 'do'
(a certain statement);

The variable i (which is known as the "controlled variable of the 'for' statement") is to be put equal to 1, and then every number in steps of 1 up to and including 50, and the subsequent statement performed for each of these values. The numbers used in a 'for' statement may be any positive or negative numbers or any variable or arithmetic expression, provided that a variable has previously been assigned a certain value. Thus:

'for' x := 3 'step' −2 'until' −99 'do'
'for' n := 1 'step' a 'until' b 'do'

In the latter case, a and b must have already been given some values.

If you write something like:

'for' b := 10 'step' 6 'until' 3 'do'

the loop will not be performed at all, because the computer will check each value against the value of the final item before proceeding.

29

The right-hand side of a **'for'** statement is called the **'for'** *list*. It may take two other forms besides the **'step'** **'until'** form already illustrated. Here are examples of the other two types of **'for'** statement.

    'for' j := 1, 3, 5, 6, 10, 25 **'do'**

In this instance the variable takes successively the listed values. Note carefully where the comma separators occur.

    'for' p := 1, p + 1 **'while'** p **'le'** a **'do'**

Here the variable takes the values from 1 upwards while the value of **p** is less than or equal to **a**.

Finally, the **'for'** list can be any combination of the three forms already shown. For example:

    'for' a := 1 **'step'** 1 **'until'** 100, 105 **'step'**
              5 **'until'** 200, 250, 300 **'do'**
    'for' b := 1, 6, 8, 11, 17, 20 **'step'** 3 **'until'**
              50 **'do'**
    'for' c := 12 **'step'** −2 **'until'** −16, c − 1 **'while'**
              c > x − y **'do'**

Note the position of the commas in all these examples. No comma ever precedes the word **'do'**.

In view of what was said in Chapter 9 about compound statements, if the operation to be performed for each value of the controlled variable consists of more than one statement, then the brackets **'begin'** and **'end'** must enclose the whole operation.

        a := sum := 0;
        'for' i := 1, i + 1 **'while'** a **'le'** 1000 **'do'**
  'begin' x := i $\uparrow$ 2 ;
          sum := sum + x ;
          a := sum $\uparrow$ 2
  'end' ;

Can you work out how many times this loop will operate?

Although the following may not be relevant to any simple programs that you might write at the moment, it may be worth bearing in mind, because it may explain certain errors that you will no doubt make on occasions.

If, during the performance of a **'for'** statement, you jump out of a loop (by means of an **'if'** and **'goto'** statement) before the **'for'** list has been completed, the controlled variable will retain the last value it was assigned.

If, however, the **'for'** list has been exhausted, the value of the controlled variable after completion is undefined. That is, it may then have any value at all and so cannot be relied on. It will therefore be useless until re-assigned a value.

15
Arrays

More often than not, our calculations require a large number of data items. If we intend to operate on each one in the same way, we could form a loop and read in each number at the beginning of the loop, process it, print the result and return for the next number.

It is much easier, however, to process the numbers as a single group or set, making use of the **'for'** statement.

We place all the numbers into a group of locations in the computer. This group or **'array'** is given a name (which is any valid identifier) and we may then refer to any item in the group by giving this name, followed by a number. The computer automatically numbers the series of items for us.

We will start with a simple single set of numbers to which we will give the name **list**. The **'array'** is declared, together with the **'integer'** and **'real'** variables, at the beginning of the program, in this way:

'array' list [1 : 50] ;

The numbers in square brackets indicate the size of the group and are known as a *bound pair*. The numbers 1 and 50 are the *bounds* of the array. On reading this declaration the computer reserves a block of fifty locations and considers them as numbered from 1 to 50. If we now refer to, say, **list [19]**, the computer will know we are referring to the nineteenth number of the series. The number **19** is called the *subscript* and the whole item, **list [19]**, is known as a *subscripted variable*. It may be used in any situation where any other variable may be used, thus:

x := list [19] ;
y := list [8] + list [9] ;
list [24] := 1·0 ;
'if' list [1] = list [2] 'then' list [2] := 0·0 ;

We can see how useful the **'for'** statement is when used in conjunction with arrays. If we wish to read in fifty numbers from the input stream and place them in the array **list**, all we need say is:

> **'for' i : = 1 'step' 1 'until' 50 'do'**
> **list [i] : = read ;**

The controlled variable **i** is first set to 1 and the first item on the input stream is assigned to the location **list [1]**. **i** is now put equal to 2 and the second number assigned to **list [2]**. And so on for all fifty numbers.

We now have our fifty numbers read in to the array and can operate on them in any desired way. For instance, suppose we wish to print the squares and cubes of these fifty numbers.

> **'for' i : = 1 'step' 1 'until' 50 'do'**
> **'begin' print (list [i] ↑ 2, 4, 4) ;**
> **print (list [i] ↑ 3, 8, 4) ;**
> **newline(2)**
> **'end' ;**

and that's it.

The array **list** which we have used as an example has one *dimension*. In other words, we completely identify any one item by quoting just one number or subscript.

Arrays may have any number of dimensions, though in practice we shall not normally need more than two. A two-dimensional array may be regarded as a rectangular block of values, having a certain number of rows and columns, both of which must have their lower and upper bounds declared.

> **'integer' 'array' table [1 : 12, 1 : 8] ;**

Note that we may have an **'integer' 'array'**, that is, one in which each item will be a whole number. (If the word **'integer'** is not used, it will be assumed that your array is **'real'**.)

The two bound pairs are separated by a comma. You may think of this array as a rectangular block of numbers which are arranged in twelve rows and eight columns. Each item must now be identified by its row and column number, *i.e.* by two subscripts, thus:

> **table [6, 4] ;**
> or **table [i, j] ;**
> or **table [b, b + 3] ;**

The first of these examples refers to the number in the sixth row and the fourth column of the group, and so on.

Now, if we want to read numbers from our data into a two-dimensional array, we do so by using two successive **'for'** statements like this:

```
'for' i := 1 'step' 1 'until' 12 'do'
'for' j := 1 'step' 1 'until' 8 'do'
   table [i,j] := read ;
```

It is important to understand just how this double **'for'** statement is processed. **i** is first set to 1. Now **j** is set to 1 and **table [1, 1]** becomes the first number on the input stream. **j** is now increased to 2 and **table [1, 2]** becomes the second number on the input stream. This continues until **table [1, 8]** has been read. The **j** statement is now exhausted and the computer returns to the **i** statement. **i** is increased to 2 and the whole range of the **j** statement is again performed. The process continues until the **i** statement is exhausted. You will thus notice that the first or outer **'for'** statement is the last to be exhausted.

Note that since only one statement follows the two **'for'** statements, no **'begin'** and **'end'** are needed.

Now suppose one wished to print this array in twelve rows of eight numbers each, with a blank line between each row. This is how it would need to be done:

```
    'for' i := 1 'step' 1 'until' 12 'do'
'begin' 'for' j := 1 'step' 1 'until' 8 'do'
          print (table [i,j], 3, 0) ;
          newline (2)
'end' ;
```

Notice here that the **j** statement operates only on the subsequent statement, *i.e.* **print**(*etc.*) so that a row of eight numbers is printed. But the **i** statement operates on the complete compound statement between **'begin'** and **'end'** so that we get a printed row and two new lines, twelve times.

Bearing this explanation in mind, try to work out the effect of the following two slight variations on the above example:

```
        'for' i := 1 'step' 1 'until' 12 'do'
        'for' j := 1 'step' 1 'until' 8 'do'
'begin' print (table [i,j], 3, 0) ;
          newline (2)
'end' ;
```

and:

```
    'for' i := 1 'step' 1 'until' 12 'do'
    'for' j := 1 'step' 1 'until' 8 'do'
     print (table [i,j], 3, 0) ;
     newline (2) ;
```

You will find this exercise quite important in learning how to set out results.

Now a few more remarks on ALGOL array facilities. Firstly, it is not necessary to start numbering an array from row or column 1. Any positive or negative integer may be the bound of an array provided that the lower number comes first. The computer will number the items consecutively from the lower to the upper bound, including the value zero if this should come within the range.

'array' vector [−4 : 10] ;

This array will contain 15 items and include one given the designation 0.

'integer''array' zz [2 : 12, 0 : 6] ;

This two-dimensional array will contain $11 \times 7 = 77$ items.

Always remember that using any subscript which is outside the declared range of an array will cause the computer to halt the program and output an error message. For example, in the above cases, you cannot refer to:

vector [11]   nor to   **zz [8, −2]**

Several arrays may be declared in the same declaration statement. If more than one array have the same dimensions and bounds, these need be stated only once, thus:

**'array' lista, listb [1 : 15] , listc [1 : 20] ,
tablex, tabley [−2 : 97, 1 : 10] ;**

Once more note carefully the positions of commas and the final semicolon.

Finally, we come to a particularly useful feature of ALGOL: the facility of declaring arrays with dynamic bounds. That is, bounds expressed as variables or expressions to which we may assign any values we choose. We may declare an array:

'array' ident [1 : m, 1 : n] ;

or   **'array' rect [1 : b, 1 : 3 * b] ;**

It must be noted, however, that before these declarations can be made, the variables **m**, **n** and **b** must already have been assigned definite values. You will remember that declarations must be made at the commencement of the program. How, then, can we assign values to the variables **m**, **n** and **b** before the declaration is made?

Without going deeply into the subject of "block structure" let us just say that a *block* is a part of a program which commences with declarations. A program may contain many blocks. Every block must commence with the word **'begin'**.

So, in order to make a declaration after we have made statements to assign the values for the dynamic bounds, we must clearly start another block, thus:

```
'begin' 'integer' m, n, b ;
        m := read ; n := read ; b := 15 ;
   'begin' 'array' ident [1 : m, 1 : n] ,
                   rect [1 : b, 1 : 3 * b] ;


                (body of program)


   'end'
'end' ;
```

The use of a second **'begin'** merely means that we must put a matching **'end'** at the end of the program.

16
More simple programs

In these programs we make use of 'for' statements and arrays.

Program 6

Given a list of numbers, read them into an array and then form a new array which contains the product of every pair of successive numbers in the first array. Print both arrays.

```
'begin' 'integer' i, k, m ;
       m : = read ;
   'begin' 'array' a [1 : m] , b [1 : m − 1] ;
          k : = m − 1 ;
          'for' i : = 1 'step' 1 'until' m 'do' a [i] : = read ;
          'for' i : = 1 'step' 1 'until' k 'do'
                b [i] : = a [i] * a [i + 1] ;
          'for' i : = 1 'step' 1 'until' m 'do'
                print (a [i], 6, 2) ;
           newline(2) ;
          'for' i : = 1 'step' 1 'until' k 'do'
                print (b [i], 6, 2)
   'end'
'end' ;
```

This program should be fairly straightforward. It has been assumed that the numbers in one array can be accommodated on one line of print-out.

It will be noted that a variable k has been introduced, having a value one less than m, and is used as the final value of two of the 'for' statements. If the expression m − 1 had been used instead, this expression would be evaluated at each execution of the loop so that the current value of the controlled variable i may be checked against it. This wastes time. Do not use an arithmetic expression for either the incremental or final item of a 'for' statement. Calculate the expression first and assign it to a single variable.

37

Program 7

You are presented with a list of different whole numbers. Write a general program to find the numerically greatest number. Print its value (signed) and the position it occupies in the list.

```
'begin' 'integer' i, j, k, m ;
      m : = read ;
   'begin' 'integer' 'array' set [1 : m] ;
         'for' i : = 1 'step' 1 'until' m 'do' set [i] : = read ;
         j : = abs(set [1]) ; k : = 1 ;
         'for' i : = 2 'step' 1 'until' m 'do'
         'if' abs(set [i]) > j 'then'
      'begin' j : = abs(set [i]) ;
            k : = i ;
      'end' ;
         print(set [k], 4, 0) ;
         print (k, 4, 0)
   'end'
'end' ;
```

NOTES:

1. We want the *numerically* greatest number. If we did not use the **abs** function then negative numbers, whatever their magnitude, would be considered less than any positive number.

2. We need the signed value of the greatest number. Note therefore that we must print **set [k]**, not **j**, which is its absolute value.

3. The statement **k : = i** keeps a running record of the position of the greatest number found.

4. Why is it necessary to give **k** the initial value 1? Think that one out for yourself.

Program 8

You have a daily sales list comprising two columns. The first gives the number of articles sold and the second a code number for the article, ranging from 1 to 20, say. You also have a price list for the articles. Write a program to calculate the total cash taken daily and the average taking per article sold.

```
'begin' 'integer' a, i, m, n, sumart ;
      'real' sumc, avcost ;
      m : = read ;
```

```
'begin' 'integer' 'array' sales [1 : m, 1 : 2] ;
        'array' cost [1 : 20] ;
        'for' i := 1 'step' 1 'until' m 'do'
        'for' n := 1, 2 'do' sales [i, n] := read ;
        'for' i := 1 'step' 1 'until' 20 'do' cost [i] := read ;
        sumc := 0·0 ; sumart := 0 ;
        'for' i := 1 'step' 1 'until' m 'do'
   'begin' a := sales [i, 2] ;
           sumart := sumart + sales [i, 1] ;
           sumc := sumc + sales [i, 1] * cost [a]
   'end' ;
        avcost := sumc / sumart ;
        print(sumc, 4, 2) ; print(avcost, 3, 3)
   'end'
'end' ;
```

This program is rather more tricky. Array **sales** contains two columns, one for the number of articles sold and the second for the code number. For each item, first extract the code number, *i.e.* **sales [i, 2]**, and put it equal to **a**. Then **cost [a]** locates the appropriate price. This was not strictly necessary but it is possibly a little easier to follow than:

sumc := sumc + sales [i, 1] * cost [sales [i, 2]] ;

which is, in fact, equivalent to what has been done.

Program 9

Write a program to extract the cube root of any given positive number by the following iterative method:

1. Choose any trial root, t. Say $t = 8$.

2. Divide the number by t and find the square root, r, of the quotient.

3. Find the average of t and r and use it as the next trial root.

4. Continue the process until the latest and previous roots differ by less than 0·0001.

```
'begin' 'integer' i ;
        'real' n, t, new, q, r ;
        n := read ;
        new := 8·0 ;
        'for' i := 1, i + 1 'while' abs(t − new) > 0·0001 'do'
```

```
'begin' t := new ;
        q := n / t ;
        r := sqrt(q) ;
        new := (t + r) / 2
'end' ;
        print(new, 4, 4)
 'end' ;
```

The best way to understand what is going on in this program is to choose a number and follow the program through statement by statement. It should then become clear.

One point requires explanation. It may be thought that in the **'for' 'while'** statement, for the first time through, the value of **abs(t − new)** cannot be tested because **t** has not yet been assigned a value. However, in a **'for' 'while'** statement, the first value, before the comma, is not so tested, only the subsequent values. On the other hand, the variable **new** must be assigned in view of the first statement in the loop, **t := new;**

If one wants every value of the controlled variable to be tested in a **'for' 'while'** statement, one must proceed thus:

```
i := 0 ;
'for' i := i + 1 'while' (condition) 'do'
```

Program 10

Read in a series of positive numbers and print them in descending order of magnitude. (This program is somewhat similar to Program 7, but also shows how to sort numbers. You may find this useful in many other programs.) First, let us construct a flow diagram (*see* Fig. 3).

Note that, in the program which follows, the loops are formed by using **'for'** statements, which is usual. It is clearer and more convenient, however, in a flow diagram, to indicate loops as shown, rather in the manner which we adopted prior to Chapter 14.

```
'begin' 'integer' i, j, k, m, n ; 'real' t, x ;
        n := read ;
 'begin' 'array' a [1 : n] ;
        'for' i := 1 'step' 1 'until' n 'do' a [i] := read ;
        k := n − 1 ;
        'for' i := 1 'step' 1 'until' k 'do'
```

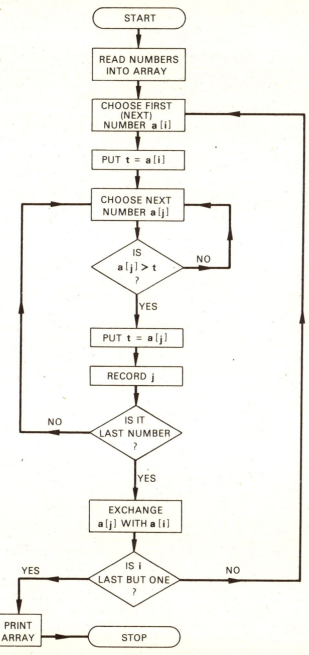

FIG. 3. Flow diagram for Program 10.

```
      'begin' t := a [i] ;
            'for' j := i + 1 'step' 1 'until' n 'do'
            'if' a [j] > t 'then'
         'begin' t := a [j] ;
               m := j
      'end' ;
            x := t ; a [m] := a [i] ; a [i] := x
   'end' ;
         'for' i := 1 'step' 1 'until' n 'do'
         print(a [i], 3, 2)
   'end'
'end' ;
```

Note that a straight "swap" of two numbers must be done by using a reserve location, in this case x.

Program 11

Given a list of test results, calculate their average. If any result shows more than a 5% deviation from the accepted average, it must be rejected. Print the accepted average and the number of results on which it is based. (Note: An iterative method is called for here, since the rejection of any result will immediately modify the average which may lead, in turn, to more rejections.)

```
'begin' 'integer' i, j, k, m ; 'real' av, newav, sum ;
      m := read ;
   'begin' 'array' a [1 : m] ;
         'for' i := 1 'step' 1 'until' m 'do' a [i] := read ;
         sum := 0·0 ;
         'for' i := 1 'step' 1 'until' m 'do'
         sum := sum + a [i] ;
         av := sum / m ;
         'for' j := 1, j + 1 'while' j > 0 'do'
      'begin' k := 0 ; sum := 0·0 ;
         'for' i := 1 'step' 1 'until' m 'do'
         'if' a [i] > 0·95 * av 'or' a [i] < 1·05 * av 'then'
      'begin' k := k + 1 ;
            sum := sum + a [i]
      'end' ;
         'if' k = 0 'then' 'goto' noresult ;
         newav := sum / k ;
         'if' abs(newav − av) < 0·001 'then' 'goto' stop ;
         av := newav
```

```
      'end' ;
stop:       print(newav, 3, 3) ;
            print(k, 2, 0) ;
noresult:
   'end'
'end' ;
```

NOTES:

1. The **'for' 'while'** statement used here is one way of intro-ducing a loop when the programmer does not know initially how many times the loop may need to be used. You will notice that, taken by itself, this statement is endless. An end is reached, however, when **abs(newav − av) < 0·001**, in other words when two successive runs of the loop give an identical average. Then the program proceeds to the label **stop:** which is outside the loop.

2. Variable **k** counts the number of results included in the sum, in order to calculate the average. Note that there is a possibility that *every* result falls outside the permitted range of 5%. We must therefore guard against the error of dividing by zero, by testing **k** and providing an exit if it is zero.

Program 12

Print *in triangular form* Pascal's triangle, which gives the binomial coefficients of $(1 + x)^n$ up to $n = 12$, thus:

```
                1
            1       1
        1       2       1
    1       3       3       1                etc.
```

The problem is simply stated but perhaps not quite so simple to program. Each coefficient is the sum of the numbers to each side in the row above, except the first and last which are equal to 1. The reader may like to check for himself that the following program does the trick.

```
'begin' 'integer' i, j;
        'integer' 'array' pasc [1 : 12, 1 : 12] ;
        'for' i : = 1 'step' 1 'until' 12 'do'
'begin' 'for' j : = 1 'step' 1 'until' i 'do'
        pasc [i, j] : = 'if' j = 1 'or' j = i 'then' 1
        'else' pasc [i − 1, j − 1] + pasc [i − 1, j]
```

```
      'end' ;
         'for' i : = 1 'step' 1 'until' 12 'do'
     'begin' space(60 − 3 * i) ;
            'for' j : = 1 'step' 1 'until' i 'do'
              print(pasc [i,j],3,0); newline(2)
      'end'
   'end' ;
```

17
The writetext statement and page layout

We usually want to incorporate page titles or column headings into our results, or simply to write explanatory notes on the results. We can do this with the **writetext** statement. A few examples will illustrate its use.

writetext ('('table%of%results')') ;

A **writetext** statement, as you see, is enclosed within normal round brackets **( )** and within these are "string quotes" **'(' ')'** Everything within the string quotes is reproduced exactly as written, except that the symbol **%** must be inserted if we want a blank space. The result of making the above statement would be the output:

TABLE OF RESULTS

The statement:

writetext ('('values%of%2%*%(y + z).')') ;

would similarly result in the output:

VALUES OF 2 * (Y + Z).

It is probable that sometimes you may write:

writetext ('('class averages for group a')') ;

and you will get the unintended mess:

CLASSAVERAGESFORGROUPA

Remember that you *must* tell the computer you want a blank space by inserting **%** You may recall that when the computer *reads* any program statement it will ignore all spaces.

There are three special letters we may also include within a **writetext** statement. They are known as *layout editing characters*. They are:

p   paperthrow   Printer goes to the head of a new page.

c	newline	Printer starts a new line.
s	space	Printer outputs one blank space.

If **c** or **s** is preceded by an unsigned integer then you will get that number of new lines or spaces.

When one or more of these characters appears within a **writetext** statement they must be enclosed within their own string quotes, thus:

writetext('("('p')'batch%a'('2c3s')'sub-set%d')') ;

which would result in the following output at the head of a new page:

BATCH A

SUB-SET D

These editing characters produce exactly the same effect as the statements:

paperthrow ;
newline(n) ; ⎫
space(n) ; ⎬ These two we have come across already.
         ⎭

Thus, the statement:

writetext('("('p2c3s')')')') ;

would give precisely the same output as:

paperthrow ; newline(2) ; space(3) ;

There are 120 spaces per line and 50 lines per page of the normal line-printer output. The line-printer will automatically take a new line after 120 spaces and a new page after 50 lines.

```
                    EXAMINATION RESULTS.

NAME        NO.     ENGLISH   FRENCH   MATHEMATICS   PHYSICS

```

```
             INVENTORY OF EQUIPMENT.
             -----------------------

MATHEMATICS DEPARTMENT
-----------------------

ROOM        CHAIRS      DESKS      TABLES      CALCULATORS
```

FIG. 4. Output using **writetext** statement.

With this information and that already given about the printing format output by the statement **print(p,m,n);** you should now be able to set out your results neatly. A piece of graph paper comes in handy when you are planning the layout.

Do not confuse the **print** and **writetext** statements. **print** only prints numbers which are stored in named locations. **writetext** writes whatever is within the statement, whether it be letters, numbers or symbols.

You could practise setting-out the two examples shown in Fig. 4.

18
Boolean variables and expressions

There is another type of variable which has not hitherto been mentioned. It is known as a **'boolean'**. Such a variable cannot be assigned a numerical value but merely the "values" **'true'** and **'false'**. These variables sometimes provide a convenient way of carrying out a simple test at various points in a program. The declaration of a **'boolean'** variable is made in just the same way as an **'integer'**, **'real'** or **'array'**, at the commencement of the program, thus:

$$\text{'boolean' } z, \text{ found ;}$$

This simply means that the variables **z** and **found** will be assigned not numerical values but the values **'true'** or **'false'**. The values assigned may be the actual words **'true'** or **'false'** or any arithmetic relation (which is a form of **'boolean'** expression). For instance:

$$z := a = b ;$$

The variable **z** will be put equal to **'true'** if $a = b$ and **'false'** otherwise. Whatever the values of **a** and **b**, this relation must be either true or false.

$$\text{found} := p < q \text{ 'and' } q < r ;$$

The variable **found** will be given the value **'true'** only if **p** is less than **q** and also **q** is less than **r**, in other words only if **p, q** and **r** are in ascending order of magnitude.

$$\text{odd} := t = 1 \text{ 'or' } t = 3 \text{ 'or' } t = 5 ;$$

In this case, if variable **t** has the value 1 or 3 or 5 then **odd** will be put equal to **'true'**, otherwise **'false'**.

We have seen, in dealing with **'if'** statements, that the word **'if'** is always followed by some relation. This relation can therefore be replaced by a **'boolean'** variable.

$$\text{'if' } q \text{ 'then' } a := 1 \text{ 'else' } a := 2 ;$$

which simply means: if **q** has the value **'true'** then . . . etc. Better still, we could write the conditional assignment statement:

$$a := \text{'if' } q \text{ 'then' } 1 \text{ 'else' } 2 \; ;$$

The sort of situation in which a **'boolean'** may be found useful can be illustrated by the following example.

Suppose that several times in a program we wish to do something provided two variables fulfil certain conditions, say:

$$a \text{ 'le' } 0\cdot0 \text{ 'and' } b < x \uparrow 2 - y \uparrow 2$$

We don't want to keep writing this out in full, so we can declare a **'boolean'** variable **ab** and assign it thus:

$$ab := a \text{ 'le' } 0\cdot0 \text{ 'and' } b < x \uparrow 2 - y \uparrow 2 \; ;$$

Whenever we come to test for this condition, we simply say:

$$\text{'if' } ab \text{ 'then'} \quad \text{etc.}$$

It will be found that, except in advanced programming, the use of **'boolean'** variables is not often required. The same result can be achieved, indeed, by assigning one of two simple numerical values to an **'integer'** variable.

19
Procedures

In extensive programs, we often require to carry out a series of operations many times in the program, or to calculate a rather complex function and use it several times. In order to avoid having to write the whole operation each time that we need it, the operation or function may be prepared as a smaller subsidiary program (or **'procedure'**) and "called" into operation at any point in the program.

Let us start with a very simple process, that of assigning zero values to all the elements of a one-dimensional array. If this were done only once in the body of the program we should write this:

> **'for'** i : = 1 **'step'** 1 **'until'** n **'do'**
>   vector [i] : = 0 ;

We shall now write this as a **'procedure'** and then explain its construction and vital points.

> **'procedure'** clear(a, m); **'array'** a ; **'integer'** m;
>   **'begin' 'integer'** i ;
>   **'for'** i : = 1 **'step'** 1 **'until'** m **'do'**
>   a [i] : = 0
>   **'end'** ;

1. The **'procedure'** is first given a name, which can be any valid identifier. In this case, we have chosen the name **clear**.

2. The name is now followed in round brackets by a list of the "formal parameters." These are the essential facts required to carry out the operation. Here we need to know the name of the array to be cleared and how many elements it contains. That's all.

3. Following these, we declare what type of variable each parameter represents. Here, **a** is to be an **'array'** and **m** an **'integer'**.

4. Now follow the details of the operation, bracketed by **'begin'** and **'end'** only if the operation contains more than one statement (including internal declarations).

50

5. In this example we need a counter for the controlled variable of the 'for' statement, so 'begin' is followed by the declaration of an 'integer' i.

6. Note particularly that a 'procedure' as written is simply a declaration. It does not instruct the computer to do anything at all, any more than does the declaration 'integer' z; We are merely giving notice that we intend to use a 'procedure' bearing the name **clear** and defining what we mean by it.

Now having declared the 'procedure' how do we use it? Simply by calling its name and telling the computer the actual values (*actual parameters*) which we want it to use, that is, stating the name of the array we want cleared and the number of elements in it. For example:

clear(vector,15) ;

When this call is encountered, the actual parameters, **vector** and **15** are substituted for the formal parameters, **a** and **m**, wherever they occur in the procedure instructions. The computer will thus actually do:

```
'for' i := 1 'step' 1 'until' 15 'do'
    vector [i] := 0 ;
```

We may substitute any declared array for **a** and any number, arithmetic expression or variable for **m** (provided that the expression or variable has been given a definite value at the time we make the call and that of course the value is consistent with the declared bounds of the array).

One point to note about the parameters and other internally declared variables is that they have a significance only within the procedure. They will therefore not conflict with any variables of the same name used in the program itself. This is quite an advantage, because it means that if we are using several procedures, the total number of identifiers used in the program is not increased in any way.

Let us now see how we could increase the scope of our procedure and use it to set any consecutive elements of the array to zero, not necessarily all of them. We must now include in our essential information the first and last items to be dealt with. These must be made formal parameters of the procedure. Call them **ia** and **ib**. We do not now need **m**.

```
'procedure' clear(a, ia, ib) ; 'array' a ;
            'integer' ia, ib ;
     'begin' 'integer' i ;
            'for' i := ia 'step' 1 'until' ib 'do'
                a [i] := 0
     'end' ;
```

The call: **clear(vector, 2, 12)** ; will put all the elements from **vector [2]** to **vector [12]** equal to zero.

Further, why restrict the procedure to assigning zero values? Why, indeed? We could make it assign any value we want, provided that we are assigning the *same* value to all the elements concerned. We must make the required value another parameter, say **x**. And what about a more meaningful name for our new procedure? Let's call it **assign**.

```
'procedure' assign (a, ia, ib, x) ; 'array' a;
            'integer' ia, ib; 'real' x;
    'begin' 'integer' i ;
            'for' i := ia 'step' 1 'until' ib 'do'
                a [i] := x
    'end' ;
```

And so on *ad infinitum*. (Almost!)

Let us now try something quite different. Given a number of values, we wish to read them direct from the data stream, calculate their sum and their average and output the answers to two stated variables. What are the essential parameters? Clearly, the number of values to be read, and in this case, two parameters to indicate where the answers are to be put.

```
'procedure' summean(m, x, y) ; 'integer' m; 'real' x, y;
    'begin' 'integer' i ;
            x := 0·0;
            'for' i := 1 'step' 1 'until' m 'do'
            x := x + read ;
            y := x / m
    'end' ;
```

A possible call might be:

summean(20, e, f) ;

This will read twenty numbers from the input stream, assign their sum to variable **e** and their average to variable **f**.

summean(48, list [m], record [6, 6]) ;

This call will read forty-eight values, place their sum in array **list** as item **m**, and their average in array **record**, in row 6 and column 6.

Before we go further, try writing procedures for the following operations.

1. Given the values a, b and c in the equation $ax^2 + bx + c = 0$, output the two roots of the quadratic. (Assume for the

sake of simplicity that the roots will always be real, not imaginary.)

2. Given a two-dimensional array which is square and of any size, output the sum and product of the values on the leading diagonal, that is, the diagonal of the square running from row 1, column 1 to row m, column m.

Where a procedure is designed to give a single answer (similar to **sin(a)** or **arctan(a)** etc.) we may write what is known as a "function procedure." The declaration is now preceded by the word **'integer'** or **'real'** according to the type of the value of the function.

In a function procedure, the last statement assigns the required value to a variable bearing the same name as the procedure itself.

A simple example would be a procedure to calculate the value of some trigonometric function not already provided by the computer, *e.g.* **cosh**, the hyperbolic cosine.

```
'real' 'procedure' cosh(a) ; 'real' a;
    cosh := (exp(a) + exp( −a))/2;
```

No **'begin'** and **'end'** are necessary here because the procedure consists of only one statement. We may now use the call **cosh(a)** just like a variable:

```
y := 4 * cosh(x) ;
z := z + sqrt(cosh(m)) ;
```

Another simple example is a procedure for calculating the length of the hypotenuse of a right-angled triangle:

```
'real' 'procedure' pythagoras(a,b) ; 'real' a,b;
    pythagoras := sqrt(a * a + b * b) ;
```

We might now call:

```
'for' i := 1 'step' 1 'until' 10 'do'
    a [i] := pythagoras(i, 10) ;
```

What answers would you expect to find in array **a**?

What about a procedure for calculating the area of a triangle, the lengths of the three sides being given. (It is here assumed that the triangle is "possible," *i.e.* that the sum of any two sides is greater than the third.)

```
'real' 'procedure' triarea(a, b, c); 'real' a, b, c;
    'begin' 'real' s;
            s := (a + b + c)/2;
        triarea := sqrt(s * (s−a)*(s−b)*(s−c))
    'end' ;
```

The use of an intermediate variable **s** merely obviates the need for a very long-winded expression for **triarea**. Since we have an internal declaration and two statements we need to use **'begin'** and **'end'**.

Finally an integer procedure to record the *position* of the minimum value of the elements of any array. The array name and the number of elements in it must be the parameters of the procedure.

```
'integer' 'procedure' mini(a, m); 'array' a ;
        'integer' m ;
   'begin' 'integer' i, k; 'real' x ;
           x := a [1] ; k := 1 ;
           'for' i := 2 'step' 1 'until' m 'do'
           'if' a [i] < x 'then'
      'begin' x := a [i] ; k := i
      'end' ;
           mini := k
   'end' ;
```

20
Here and there

Here are a few odd items which may be of interest and occasional use.

Integer division

Here we introduce an operational symbol not mentioned before: '/' It may be used *only* between two '**integer**' numbers or variables. The result will be an '**integer**', the actual value being rounded towards zero, *i.e.* the decimal portion is simply cut off.

10 '/' 3	gives	3
11 '/' 3	gives	3
−8 '/' 5	gives	−1

The author has found this facility useful on many occasions for deriving irregular series. Suppose, when x takes the integer values from 1 to 5, we wish to define a function $f(x)$ which will take the values 1, 4, 2, 5 and 3 respectively. By normal algebraic curve-fitting processes we have to form five simultaneous equations and solve them. The answer is:

$$f(x) = \tfrac{1}{6}(-222 + x(423 + x(-250 + x(60 - 5x))))$$

and takes some ten minutes to calculate, if not longer.
Now try it this way:

For $x = 1$	$f(x) = 1 = 3 - 2 = 3 \times 1 - 2 \times 1$

For $x = 1$	$f(x) = 1$	$= 3$	$- 2$	$= 3 \times 1$	$- 2 \times 1$
2	4	6	2	2	1
3	2	6	4	2	2
4	5	9	4	3	2
5	3	9	6	3	3
				(*a*)	(*b*)

Now, the series labelled *a* and *b* may be generated very quickly by integer division expressions, thus:

$$a := (x + 2) \; '/' \; 2 \; ;$$
$$b := (x + 1) \; '/' \; 2 \; ;$$
$$fx := 3 * a - 2 * b \; ;$$

How's that? It takes about thirty seconds (when you get the knack).

Comment

You may find it helpful to introduce at certain points in your program some remarks about the various operations going on. Some time later you may forget how the program worked and these comments will remind you. It is possible to introduce these remarks without the computer taking any notice of them, by use of the facility '**comment**'. To explain, we will rewrite Program 3 in Chapter 12.

```
'begin' 'comment' program to find triangular/square
                  numbers ;
        'integer' a, b, c ;
                  a := b := 0 ;
again:            a := a + 1 ; b := b + a ;
                  'comment' b is now triangular ;
                  'if' b > 10000 'then' 'goto' stop ;
                  c := sqrt(b) ;
                  'if' c * c = b 'then' print(b, 5, 0) ;
                  'comment' if not, b is not square ;
                  'goto' again ;
    stop:
'end' of the program ;
```

You will notice that there are three positions in which '**comment**' may be introduced.

1. After '**begin**' and introduced by '**comment**'.
2. After any semicolon and introduced by '**comment**'.
3. After any '**end**' and before the semicolon.

The computer ignores any words between '**comment**' and the *following* semicolon. Similarly between '**end**' and the following semicolon.

'switch' declarations

In dealing with **'goto'** statements, we discussed only the simple unconditional jump effected by the statement **'goto'** followed by a label. We can, however, jump to various different places in the program according to the value of an integer variable by means of a **'switch'** declaration.

Suppose, for instance, that our results are to be headed by one of three alternative page titles, *e.g.* CURRENT, VOLTAGE or RESISTANCE. We declare a **'switch'** thus, (at the commencement of a block as for other declarations):

'switch' title : = curr, volt, res ;

The name **title** is at our discretion and **curr**, **volt** and **res** will be labels somewhere in the program. This list of labels can be of any length. At the appropriate point in the program we call:

'goto' title [m] ;

(note the *square* brackets) and a jump will take place to:

> **curr** if **m** has the value 1
> **volt** if **m** has the value 2
> **res**   if **m** has the value 3

The labelled statements could be something like:

curr: writetext('('current(amps)')'); 'goto' next ;
volt: writetext('('voltage(millivolts)')'); 'goto' next ;
res: writetext('('resistance(ohms)')') ;
next: following statement ;

Notice that unless the statement **'goto' next** is included as shown, the computer will carry on and write the subsequent titles *as well*. The computer does not skip a statement just because it has a label.

Another example is afforded by the solution of a quadratic equation. According to whether the value of b^2 is less than, equal to or greater than the value of $4ac$, we may wish to print the results with some appropriate comment as to the real or imaginary nature of the roots.

We might declare the following **'switch'**:

'switch' calc : = le, eq, gr ;

Now there is an interesting and sometimes very useful function, **sign**(x), which takes the value -1 when x is negative, 0 when $x = 0$ and 1 when x is positive. Thus, the expression:

sign(b * b − 4 * a * c)

must yield the values -1, 0 or 1. If we add 2 to the above expression, we shall get 1, 2, or 3. So the call:

'goto' calc [sign(b * b $-$ 4 * a * c) + 2] ;

will cause a jump to the labels le: eq: or gr:

entier(n)

This is one standard function, not included in Chapter 7, which gives the nearest whole number which is *not greater* than n. Thus:

entier(9·76)	gives	9
entier($-4\cdot2$)	gives	-5

(Note: -4 is greater than $-4\cdot2$.)

It is difficult to state a common use for functions like sign and entier. One can only say that in program-writing one will occasionally come across a situation where the neatest solution to a problem is afforded by the use of one of these "unusual" facilities. A neat use of the function sign has already been mentioned. Here is an example of how entier has been used by the author recently.

It was required to title certain pages of experimental results with the date of the experiment, together with other information. For the sake of simplicity we will say that we need the date and the magnitude of the load applied to a model structure, which may range from zero to 50 newtons. There being many such pages of results, a single key number was entered on the data for each page and the following procedure used:

```
'procedure' title(k); 'integer' k ;
    'begin' 'integer' b, e, g ; 'real' a, c, d, f ;
            a := k / 10 ⬆ 4 ; b := entier(a) ;
            c := a − b ; d := 100 * c ; e := entier(d) ;
            f := d − e ; g := 100 * f ;
    writetext('('date%%%')'); print(b,2,0);
    writetext('('/%')'); print(e,2,0);
    writetext('('/%71')'); space(10);
    writetext('('load')'); print(g,2,0);
    writetext('('newtons')')
    'end' ;
```

It will be found that a value for k of 241025 will produce the title:

DATE   24 / 10 / 71   LOAD 25 NEWTONS

Similarly the key number 30100 would give:

DATE   3 / 1 / 71   LOAD 0 NEWTONS

It is recognised that there would be many ways of achieving the same object.

21
Complete programs with data

We have mentioned the provision of data for most programs and described the form it must take. We now give two complete programs requiring data, showing the form they take in order to be processed in the computer (*see* Figs. 5 and 6).

Certain preliminary instructions must be given identifying the name of the user and the program. The computer centre would tell you what these are. The examples given use typical instruction lines.

Programs may be prepared either on paper tape or on cards. The special control instructions will normally be on separate cards or separated by a new line on paper tape, but in ALGOL

```
JOB BILLBLOGGS,S12TABCX, ROYAL GS
LALGOL PR51
****
DOC SOURCE PR51
'BEGIN' 'COMMENT' THIS PROGRAM PRINTS EVERY ODD PRIME NUMBER
                 UP TO A CERTAIN LIMIT WHICH IS READ IN AS
                 DATA;
        'INTEGER' A,B,D,M,N;
         M:= READ;
         'FOR' N:= 3 'STEP' 2 'UNTIL' M 'DO'
  'BEGIN'  D:= 1;
          'FOR' D:= D + 2 'WHILE' D 'LE' SQRT(N) 'DO'
       'BEGIN' 'COMMENT' IT IS NECESSARY ONLY TO TEST DIVISIBILITY
                   BY EVERY PRIME UP TO SQRT(N) BUT HERE WE
                   DIVIDE BY EVERY ODD NUMBER TO SIMPLIFY
                   THE 'FOR' STATEMENT;
             A:= N / D;
             B:= D * A;
             'IF' N = B 'THEN' 'GOTO' NEXTNO
        'END' OF DIVISORS;
          PRINT(N,5,0);
NEXTNO:
    'END' OF EACH NUMBER TESTED
'END';
****
DOC DATA PR51
1000
****
end of tape symbol or blank cards
```

FIG. 5. Program to print prime numbers.

```
JOB ABCSMITH,X35YABCS,CENTREA
LALGOL PR22
****
DOC SOURCE PR22
'BEGIN' 'COMMENT' THIS PROGRAM READS IN ANY 16 NUMBERS INTO
                  A 4 BY 4 MATRIX (ARRAY) AND DIVIDES EACH
                  NUMBER BY THE AVERAGE VALUE OF THE ELEMENTS
                  ON THE LEADING DIAGONAL;
        'INTEGER' I,J; 'REAL'  Z; 'ARRAY'    A[1:4,1:4];
        'FOR' I:= 1,2,3,4 'DO'   'FOR' J:=    1,2,3,4   'DO'
             A[I,J]:= READ;
         Z:= 0.0;
         'FOR' I:= 1,2,3,4 'DO'  Z:= Z + ABS(A[I,I]);
         Z:= Z/4;
         'IF' Z 'LE' 0.000001   'THEN'
     'BEGIN' WRITETEXT('('''('P2C') 'DIVISOR%ALMOST%ZERO.%
                    PROBLEM%ABANDONED`)');
            'GOTO' OUT
     'END'
          'ELSE'
     'BEGIN' PAPERTHROW; NEWLINE(2);
            'FOR' I:= 1,2,3,4 'DO' 'FOR'   J:= 1,2,3,4  'DO'
                 A[I,J]:= A[I,J] / Z
     'END';
         'FOR' I:= 1,2,3,4 'DO'
     'BEGIN''FOR' J:= 1,2,3,4 'DO' PRINT(A [I,J],6,3);
            NEWLINE(2)
     'END';     OUT:
'END';
****
DOC DATA PR22
24.5  0.67  -86.3  245  1.675  19.23  7.26  101.8  24
60.87  92.564  17.55  33.3  123.45  71  59.983
****
end of tape symbol or blank cards
```

FIG. 6. Program for a matrix calculation

there is no need to put each program statement on a new card or line.

When you are using cards, however, there is an upper limit of 72 characters (including spaces) on the length of a program line and 80 characters for a line of data.

Appendix

The following are the answers to exercises and random questions posed in the text.

CHAPTER 3
(b) Too large an integer.
(d) No digit after decimal.
(h) Non-integral exponent after **&**.
(j) No digit after decimal.
(k) Too small a real number.
   The remainder are valid.

CHAPTER 4
(a) Commences with a digit.
(b) Contains inadmissible symbol.
(c) Contains inadmissible symbols.
(h) Contains inadmissible symbol.
(k) Contains Greek letter. Inadmissible.
(m) Contains Greek letter. Inadmissible.
(o) Contains inadmissible symbol.
(p) Contains inadmissible symbol.
   The remainder are valid.

CHAPTER 5
(a) $\mathbf{a \uparrow 3 + 2*a - 7}$
(b) $\mathbf{((p + q)/2) \uparrow 2 + 4*r \uparrow 2}$
(c) $\mathbf{(x + 3*(x \uparrow 2 - 7))/(2*y + 1) \uparrow 3}$
(d) $\mathbf{a*(1 - a)*(1 + a - a \uparrow 2)}$
(e) $\mathbf{f/(1 + (l/k) \uparrow 2/6000)}$
(f) $\mathbf{(a \uparrow x + a \uparrow (-x))/2}$

CHAPTER 6
(a) (i) $\mathbf{a} = 6$; (ii) $\mathbf{b} = 14$; (iii) $\mathbf{c} = 0$;
   (iv) $\mathbf{x} = 100 \cdot 1$; (v) $\mathbf{y} = 1 \cdot 6$; (vi) $\mathbf{z} = 0 \cdot 111$.
(b) $\mathbf{a}$ will be 20. $\mathbf{b}$ will be 12.

(c) (i) Both **m** and **n** have the value 7. The 4 has been lost.

(ii) In order to effect the swap, say

$$x := m ;$$
$$m := n ;$$
$$n := x ;$$

CHAPTER 9

The relations **t** = **2** and **t** = **4** cannot both be true. The program can therefore never reach the label **result**:

CHAPTER 12

Program to find the number which is simultaneously square and square pyramidal:

```
'begin' 'integer' a, b, c, d ;
        a := b := c := 0 ;
again:  a := a + 1 ; b := a*a ; c := c + b ;
        'if' c > 10000 'then' 'goto' stop ;
        d := sqrt(c) ;
        'if' d * d = c 'then' print(c, 5, 0) ;
        'goto' again ;
    stop:
    'end' ;
```

The reader may care to put this program through the computer to find the number.

CHAPTER 14

The loop will operate five times. **a** has the successive values 0, 1, 25, 196 and 900 on entering the loop.

CHAPTER 15

The first variation leads to every number being printed on a separate line with one blank line between each.

The second variation leads to the printing of one long stream of numbers, the printer automatically jumping to a new line when the end of a line of paper is reached.

CHAPTER 16

Program 7

Suppose the first number were the greatest. Then the loop controlled by the **'if'** statement will never operate and **k** will never be assigned a value. The computer cannot then obey the instruction:

print(set [k], 4, 0);

and the program fails.

CHAPTER 17

The following will effect the layouts shown.

```
writetext('("('p2c20s')'examination%results.')');
newline(2);
writetext('('name'('9s')'no.%%%%%english%%%french
        %%%mathematics%%%physics')');
writetext('("('p2c10s')'inventory%of%equipment.
        '('c10s')"')');
'for' i := 1 'step' 1 'until' 22 'do'
writetext('(' −')'); newline(2) ;
writetext('('mathematics%department'('c')")');
'for' i := 1 'step' 1 'until' 22 'do'
writetext('(' −')') ; newline(2) ;
writetext('('room'('10s')'chairs%%%%%desks%%%%%
        tables%%%%%calculators')');
```

(Note that where fewer than eight spaces occur, it is quicker to
punch, say, %%%%% than '('5s')'.)

CHAPTER 19

```
'procedure' roots(a, b, c, x, y); 'real' a, b, c, x, y;
    'begin' x := (−b+sqrt(b*b − 4*a*c))/(2*a);
            y := (−b−sqrt(b*b − 4*a*c))/(2*a)
    'end';


'procedure' diagsumprod(a, m, sum, prod); 'array' a;
            'integer' m; 'real' sum, prod;
    'begin' 'integer' i; sum := 0·0; prod := 1·0;
            'for' i := 1 'step' 1 'until' m 'do'
        'begin' sum := sum + a [i, i] ;
                prod := prod * a [i, i]
        'end'
    'end' ;
```

Array **a** would contain the following approximate values:

10·05 10·2 10·45 10·78 11·18 11·65 12·2 12·8 13·45 14·14

Index

A

abs (x), 13
actual parameter, 51
alphabetic symbols, 2
'and', 17
answers to exercises, 62
arctan (x), 13
arithmetic expression, 8
'array', 32
    bounds, 32
    dimension, 33
assignment statement, 10
    conditional, 16
    multiple, 11

B

'begin' and **'end'**, 16
block structure, 35
'boolean' expression, 48
'boolean' variable, 48
bound pair, 32
bounds of array, 32
bounds, dynamic, 35
brackets, round, 8
brackets, square, 32

C

'comment', 56
compound statement, 16
conditional assignment,
    statement, 16
controlled variable, 29
cos (x), 13

D

data, 18
    on cards, 61
    on tape, 22
    punching of, 22
    stream, 18
dimension of array, 33
division, integer, 55
dynamic bounds, 35

E

editing characters, 45
entier (x), 58
exp (x), 13

F

'false', 48
flow diagram, 23
'for' list, 30
'for' statement, 29
formal parameter, 50

G

'goto' statement, 14

I

identifier, 6
'if' 'then' statement, 15
'if' 'then' 'else' statement, 15
input, 18
input stream, 18
'integer', 4
integer division, 55

L

label, 14
layout editing characters, 45
ln (x), 13
logarithm to base e, 13

M

multiple assignment statement, 11

N

newline (x), 22
numbers, 4
numeric symbols, 2

O

operation symbols, 2
'or', 17
output, 19

P

page layout, 45
paperthrow, 45
parameter, 13
   actual, 51
   formal, 50
print procedure, 19
priority of operational
  symbols, 8
'procedure', 50

function procedure, 53
   parameters of, 50
programs, complete, 60
punctuation symbols, 3

R

read function, 18
'real' numbers, 4
relational symbols, 2
round brackets, 8

S

sign (x), 57
sin (x), 13
space (x), 23
sqrt (x), 13
square brackets, 32
square root, 13
string quotes, 45
subscript, 32
subscripted variable, 32
'switch', 57
symbols of language, 2

T

'true', 48

W

writetext statement, 45